ALL
THAT'S
LEFT

ALL
THAT'S
LEFT

W JAMES
EHRLICH

BERNADETTE M. LEONARD, EDITOR

ISBN: 978-0-578-49881-2

Printed in the United States of America
3 5 7 9 10 8 6 4 2

Cover image credt: ESO
Book design by Roya Seradj

For Adam

ALL
THAT'S
LEFT

LOST & FOUND

If it doesn't work out
was it meant not to be

My sunken ship stomach
Your buried treasure heart

Half a hole we cannot fill
With other people's earth

WISHFUL THINKING

A feeling of disconnect

Like when the car won't start
or the TV won't turn on
We press the button
turn over the ignition again

Wishfully thinking we're not
doing it quite right
A loose connection
we secretly believe
our desire alone
can resolve

ALL THAT'S LEFT

Is that a fire hydrant handshake
Or are you just happy to see me

Wet October and I know each other well
Pride cometh before, so I'll take you as
you are

Quiet, cold, and unabashedly yourself
My pile of leaves joy

BIMETALLIC STRIP

I finally turned the heat on
Decided to stop waking up cold, damp, and miserable
As if to stop punishing myself

Closed the October windows to the
open air
Got down on all fours to find the
radiator pilot light
Lying on the ground fumbling
the only way to turn these things on

Set the thermostat to seventy and
let those dissimilar metals try to
separate from each other
Finding themselves bonded together
forced to settle for an
unsatisfying curl

At least one of us is comfortable

WHEN IT COMES

The Joshua Tree does not wait for rain
As welcome as it may be when it comes
The Joshua Tree has too much wisdom for waiting
Too much living to be done in between

A NUMBERS GAME

If two were three
and one were two
we couldn't be together
for I'd be you

SURRENDER

Too soon to tell
If this peace is a result
Of self-care and meditation
Or completely giving up

SHOES BY THE DOOR

The simple things we take for
granted
This magical mix of order and chaos

Reductionism is such a dangerous
temptation
The oversimplified idea if only
we could control all the variables

The shoes would all be straight
in pairs
And life would somehow be better

FUSION

If the stars have formed
then what about us

The chances of matter gathering
igniting itself under pressure

Cosmic diesel engines
amongst the infinitude

The piston presses inward
a tightness in its stellar chest
Solar plexus strained
until eruption

Let it burn

NOT A FORK

Have you ever tried to eat salad
with a spoon?

There's nothing wrong with the spoon

Its bowl of soup
not yet arrived

NEGLECTING MY HOUSE PLANTS

Looking on the internet
for something real

Neglecting to water my
house plants

The plants more aware than us
what is going on around them

Their backlit screen
The open sky

EMAIL QUIET

Couldn't sleep again last night
Woke up at 5am without an alarm

Three hours of peace and email quiet
Shuffling around the apartment
Wondering whether or not to go to work

Whether or not to change everything altogether

BABY TURTLES

How many things in life are like those
baby turtles

Born wet and sandy underground
No parental protection or strength of age

They scramble towards the water
An instinctive sprint towards where they need to be

Stakes for baby turtles are different
No safety of a half-life in between

WAS IT CHILDISH?

when you crawled across
the middle console of my car

to sit in my lap and
be held
to be close

was it childish?

i don't know—

but was it sweet and innocent—

 two kids holding each other
alone in the dark

CANDLE SALE

I met you on the street
where we both stopped
Because they were selling decent candles for $1

Arm to arm flirting, buying
as many candles as were allowed
The candles looked good
smelled good

How could I have known
it was a short wick
Soon to drown under its
own malleable wax

So little difference
in the beginning
Between a dying ember
an engulfing blaze

TRANSMISSION

What's the word I'm looking for

When an axle grabs a gear
or the clutch drops and the machine
catches itself out of neutral

Coupling? Engagement?
Something to do with differentials?

Well then what's the opposite

For when an organ doesn't take
and the plant doesn't root

And the engine revs without gears meshed

Surely this can't be good for anyone

16 BLOCKS

I walk 8 blocks smoking a cigarette
And 8 blocks back smoking another
To arrive home
Alone

FOR THE FIRST TIME

We would light out in my Jeep Grand Cherokee

Almost every weekend or at least on Saturday
we'd be exploring some unexpected gem

The effervescent light streaming
through the trees on that windy
road to Bolinas

The morning rain on the cabin's
tin roof in Humboldt or the
time we reached elevation and everything on
our Christmas vacation was covered in snow

Those times the road drops
into the redwoods and you can feel
it in the temperature as well as
the calm in your soul

That time at Mt. Diablo where
my brakes overheated and we
wandered around Danville
only to be delighted

We felt like natives
More than people from the land
It felt like we were wild animals
in our natural habitat

.   .   .

And although in the end
I didn't end up loving you

For the first time
I began to love myself

DATING IN LA

So many disposable cups
Thoughtlessly we discard
replace
and repeat

CAR REPAIRS

Is this what all that effort was for
So I could carry around the same books
I've wanted to read from
apartment to apartment

And if I were to be killed in a car wreck
tomorrow
I wonder if it might have been a life
better lived
If I could not afford the car repairs

GALAXIES

If there are 100 billion galaxies
in the universe
Each person could have 14 galaxies
to themselves if divided evenly
Spread out

What a lonely thought
A single person among the light
years

Better we're all crowded together
on this ant hill
Teeming with life

BOÖTES VOID

The void exists in the negative
Staring at a photo of it
has the same effect as looking
over a cliff

Scaring yourself
not that you might fall
but rather
that you may leap

The abyss has its own
gravitational pull
We can't help but want to
fill that empty space
within

TENSION (BINDS EVERYTHING)

You said there wasn't enough
sexual tension between us
to keep seeing each other

Like a loose guitar string
the effort required
to strum a note has us quickly
setting down the instrument

Too tight and you may break
the string which puts you back
in about the same position

Any attempt to make a
sound will be overwrought
A vacuum-packed attempt
All the air removed

BATHROOM TRASH CAN

How can we have the confidence
of the bathroom trash can
Never quite the right size
Always overflowing with all
sorts of undesirable gunk
from past transgressions
and the subsequent clean up
Floss hanging off the sides
like some dental office weeping willow
What the lid attempts to hide
[if one exists]
usually fails
Either stuck open, or broken
or difficult to open with a too-small foot pedal
The bathroom trash can
In most cases does nothing right
Yet remains there self-assuredly filled to the brim
Apologizing to no one

THREE LESSONS ON LOVE
FROM MY DAD

When he found on the
browser history
I had been looking at
porn in junior high

Without shame, guilt or
judgment
He simply said
"All that stuff
has nothing to do with
love"

When my sister told
my parents
She was pregnant unexpectedly
With someone who didn't
speak the same language as them

My dad came home from
work in the middle of the day
Walked in the door
Gave my mom a hug to comfort her
Poured himself a glass of milk
And told us in a straightforward voice
"Babies come when they're supposed to"

Long ago when my mom and dad were first married
And some old boyfriend was still trying to win her back

. . .

She, being the talker, must have expressed
some feeling of confusion
to my dad

His response without pressure
"If you aren't happy here with me
I wouldn't want you to stay"

My dad never told me that story

HOME

I never used to understand
why people would leave
lights on when they left

it always seemed wasteful
maybe forgetful
mostly unnecessary

lately I've begun leaving on
a lone bulb in the corner
wanting to come home

SOLITUDE

To be comfortable
in solitude
is good company

PATIENCE

Patience is a virtue
sounds so passive

What a shame to
disguise such an important action
as doing nothing

MEMORY

Many years ago
in a Wyoming field
I got out of the truck I was driving
Started walking in my above the knee waders

Right outside my periphery
A giant old tree
Bare with marble bark
Ionic column
last standing
among the ruins

As I continued walking
The whole tree
Swung to the ground
like the pendulum of a
stopped clock
abruptly started
an instant before
the bell tolls

In the moment
I heard the tree
come crashing down
I felt the age-old riddle had
been solved for me personally
Case closed

Now when I think back years later
I'm less sure
It made a sound

RELEASE

To not care in the right way
may be the most powerful
position one can take

As if not subjected to gravity
No fear of falling

Rather than hang on with
white knuckle anxiety
let go–
release–

and find yourself
weightless

UNTIL YOU'RE READY

You aren't ready to have it
until you're ready to not have it

the way we tell children
engaged in a toy tug-of-war

"Let go of it and I'll give it to you"
Is God so different

ENOUGH

As if one thing
would make everything better

Have you ever considered
you are already enough
without it

DENIAL

People can be hard to figure out
When you don't want to admit
The answer is obvious

WHAT IF IT BREAKS

Antique heart
"What if it breaks?"
you ask yourself

Handing your heart
across the table with an
eyes locked smile

DAYS WHEN DOGS LIKE ME

On days when dogs like me
I like myself better

Dogs cannot be impressed
or lied to with an
imaginary treat in a closed fist
They size you up from the
inside out
Only to approach
if you're honest and true

UNIFIED FIELD THEORY

Nature is a shy beauty
Can read your intentions
Will only tell you her secrets
If you're genuinely curious
Want to understand her better
To be closer

Mostly a matter of time
spent together
The memorable moments arise
from the mundane

Nature refuses to be
a one-night stand
Treated as a conquest
placed on a shelf
or filed away
Ever elusive as a love

FINGERS CROSSED

What is it about fingers crossed
As if we could only tie them in a knot–
Our desired outcome would be ensured

THE END

If this is a story
and you are the end
I don't want to know
the beginning

SILVER BULLETS

So many silver bullets
left unmanifested–

Their inadequacy
never realized

SELF-PUNISHMENT

There are few worse
self-punishments
Than thinking someone
Who doesn't care
about you
is worth it

ARRIVAL

How could something
great come into your life
if you keep expecting it
to be another person

BEGINNING

There's magic in beginnings
don't let reality justify
too many ends

MARY OLIVER

The good ones
Die like stars exploding
Their material far flung
In every direction all at once
How was so much brilliance
Consistently burning
Without our notice

THE RIGHT AMOUNT

If you can write more
you can also write less

TRUTH

The essence of truth is not in the
having
but in the wanting

Truth is the only place our desire
is self-justified

MSG TO SELF

Things could be so good
if you would only let them

CALL BACK

So much rejection
Are we all auditioning
for parts we don't want

COMPANY

LA becomes easier
once you realize
everyone else
is also miserable

EINSTEIN'S LOVE

Einstein loved Nature
in a way that didn't leave
room for other women

He was listening to Her
for all those years
Getting her the present
she mentioned when she
didn't think he was paying
attention—no one else was

Years spent in awe
of her beauty, her perfection
and every unexpected asymmetry
opening the door to love deeper
to understand her more fully

To be so glad she is
exactly the way she is
the way she was meant to be

more perfect by her
apparent imperfections
necessary in her seeming
inconsistencies

To only be more fully appreciated
on a deeper level and to
come back to the surface

. . .

in disbelief that
her elegance had not been
initially obvious

In his later years
he stopped loving
not because he couldn't
but because he didn't
want to deal with the
uncertainty

How sad
Not willing to love
Denying the very nature
of love
of life

DESERT MATH

Every living thing
in the desert
is a miracle
Not necessarily
defying the odds
but rather showing
them to be
altogether different
than expected

Is the green of
the roulette wheel
any less likely than
the common cactus

ENTANGLEMENT

If something as complex
as the human heart can move
based on the memory
of someone we've known

Should we really
be so surprised
the mood of an individual particle
can be determined by its
simultaneous counterpart

For space is such a shorter
distance than time
And we all have
memories of reunion

ACKNOWLEDGEMENTS

What you are holding has very much so been a collaborative effort between myself and my editor Bernadette Leonard. Little did she know when she asked me "Have you been writing?" at her son's wedding last fall it would turn into this book – funny what leads to what. She is a brilliant woman, a phenomenal editor, and no push over – the bad stuff was cut and the trust we developed around the writing allowed for many things to be let go, poems and otherwise.

A special thank you to my dear friend, Mike Benz, who provided multiple generous readings of the entire collection and whose thoughtful feedback improved several poems, especially Einstein's Love. His early encouragement of the collection and continuous creative collaboration over the years has been a great source of intellectual joy.

Additionally, I would like to thank Roya Seradj who graciously lent her design talents to create the finished book you are holding. She is a fantastic designer and was an absolute pleasure to work with.